teach me about

Getting Dressed

Copyright © 1984 by Joy Berry
Living Skills Press, Sebastopol, CA
All rights reserved.
Printed in the United States of America

No part of this book may be reproduced by any
mechanical, photographic or electronic process, or in
the form of a phonographic recording, nor may it be
stored in a retrieval system, transmitted, or otherwise be
copied for public or private use without the written
permission of the publisher.

Managing Editor: Marilyn Berry
Copy Editor: Orly Kelly
Contributing Writer: Kathleen McBride
Contributing Editors: Georgiana Burt, Radhika Miller
Design and Production: Abigail Johnston
Illustrator: Bartholomew
Composition: Curt Chelin

teach me about

Getting Dressed

By JOY BERRY

Illustrated by Bartholomew

GROLIER ENTERPRISES CORP.

I like to wear clothes.

Sometimes it is cold outside.

I do not want to be cold.

I wear clothes

to keep myself warm.

BURRR

Yes NO NO

Sometimes it is hot outside.

The sun can burn my skin.

I do not want to get sunburned.

I wear clothes

to protect myself from the sun.

Yes   NO NO

I do not want to hurt myself.

I wear clothes

to protect my body.

I do not want to hurt my feet.

I wear shoes to protect my feet.

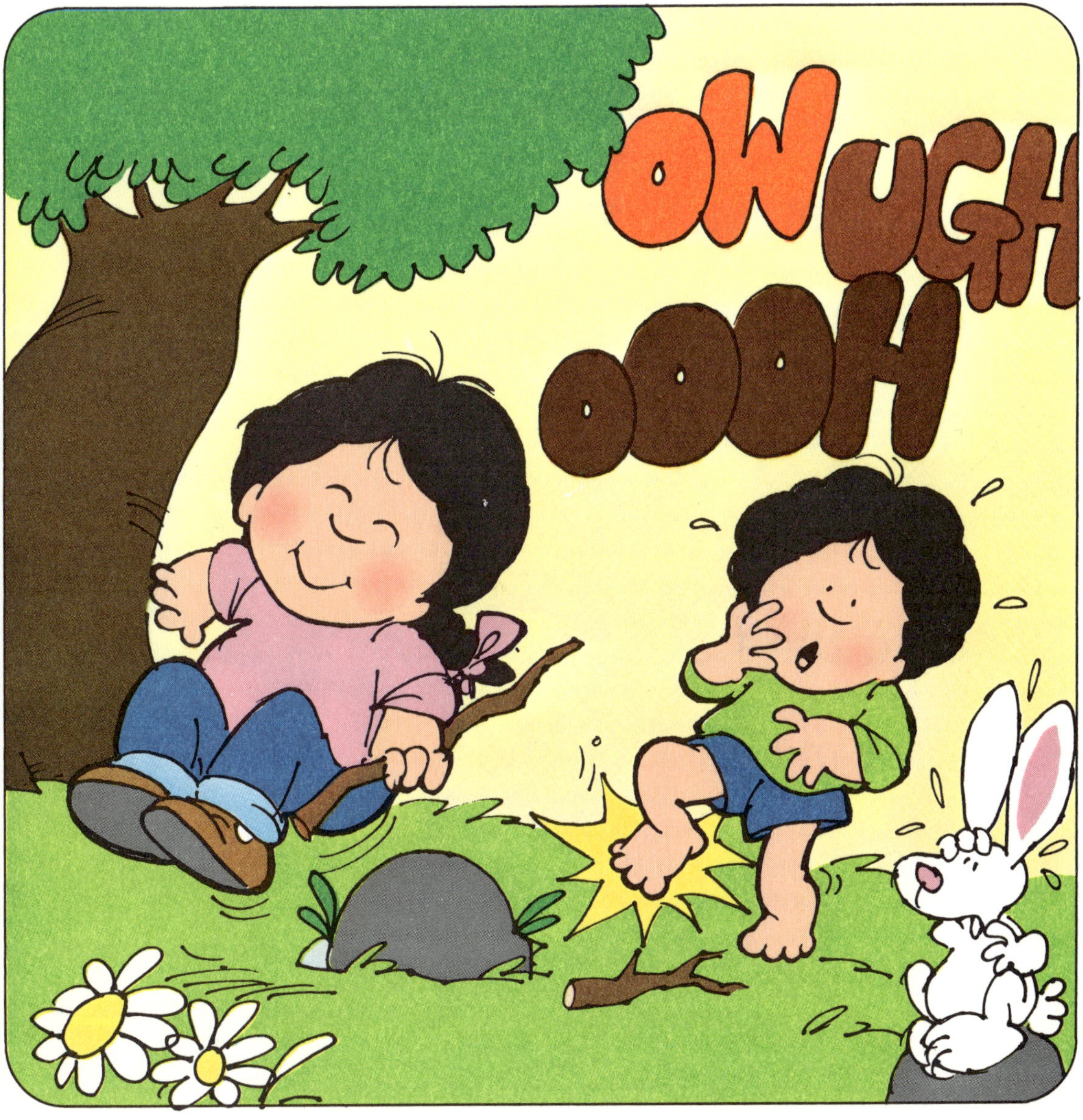
OW
UGH
OOOH

I want to take care of my clothes.

I do not want to tear them.

I do not want to

get them too dirty.

I do not throw my clothes

onto the floor.

I put my dirty clothes

into the laundry.

I put my clean clothes away.

NO NO   Yes

I am glad when

Mommy or Daddy helps me

to get dressed.

I do not run away.

I do not move around.

I help get myself dressed.

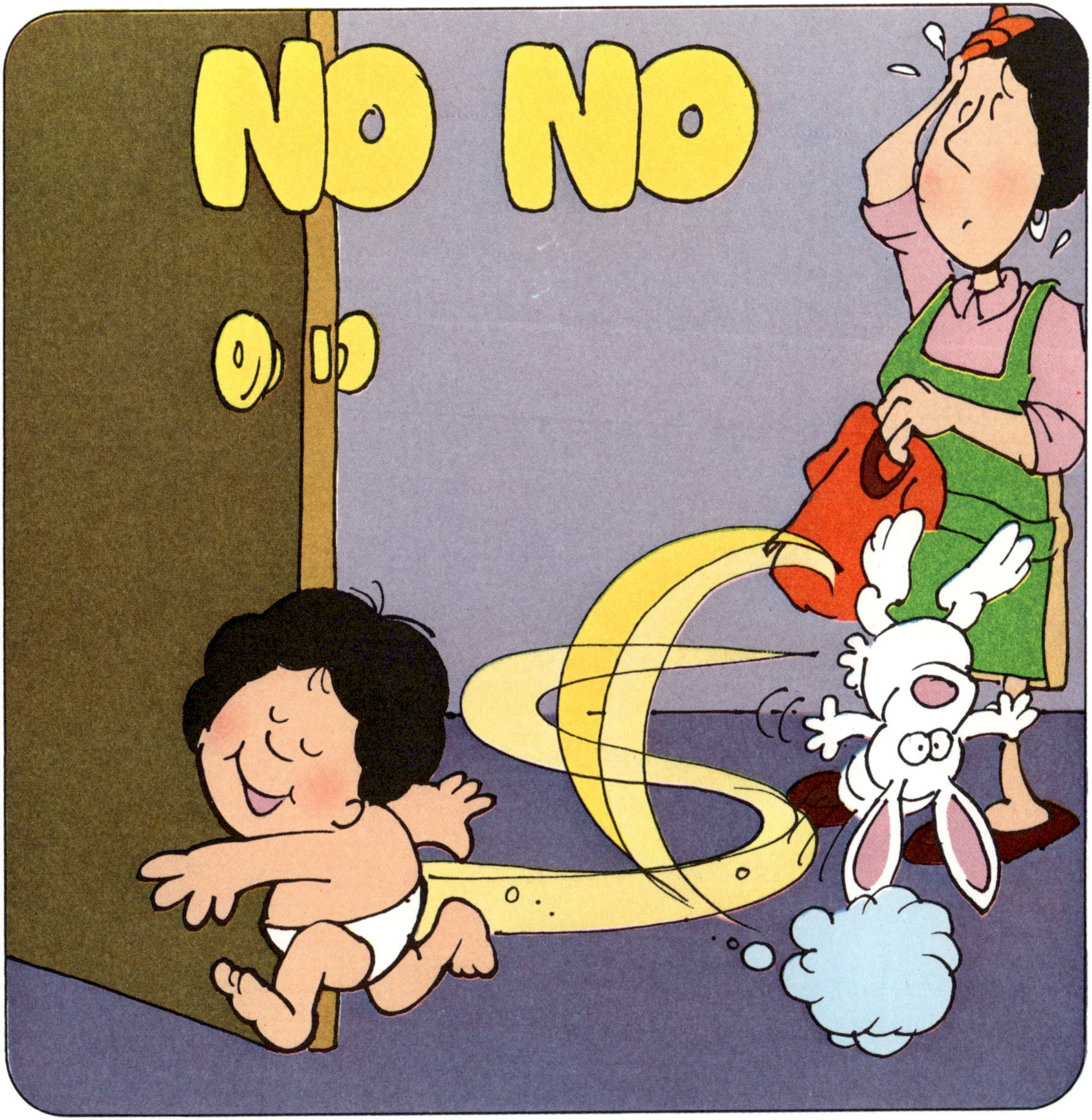
NO NO

This is the way I get dressed:

First, I put on my underpants.

Second, I put on my undershirt.

Third, I put on my top

(my shirt or blouse).

Fourth, I put on my socks.

Fifth, I put on my bottoms

(my pants or skirt).

Last, I put on my shoes.

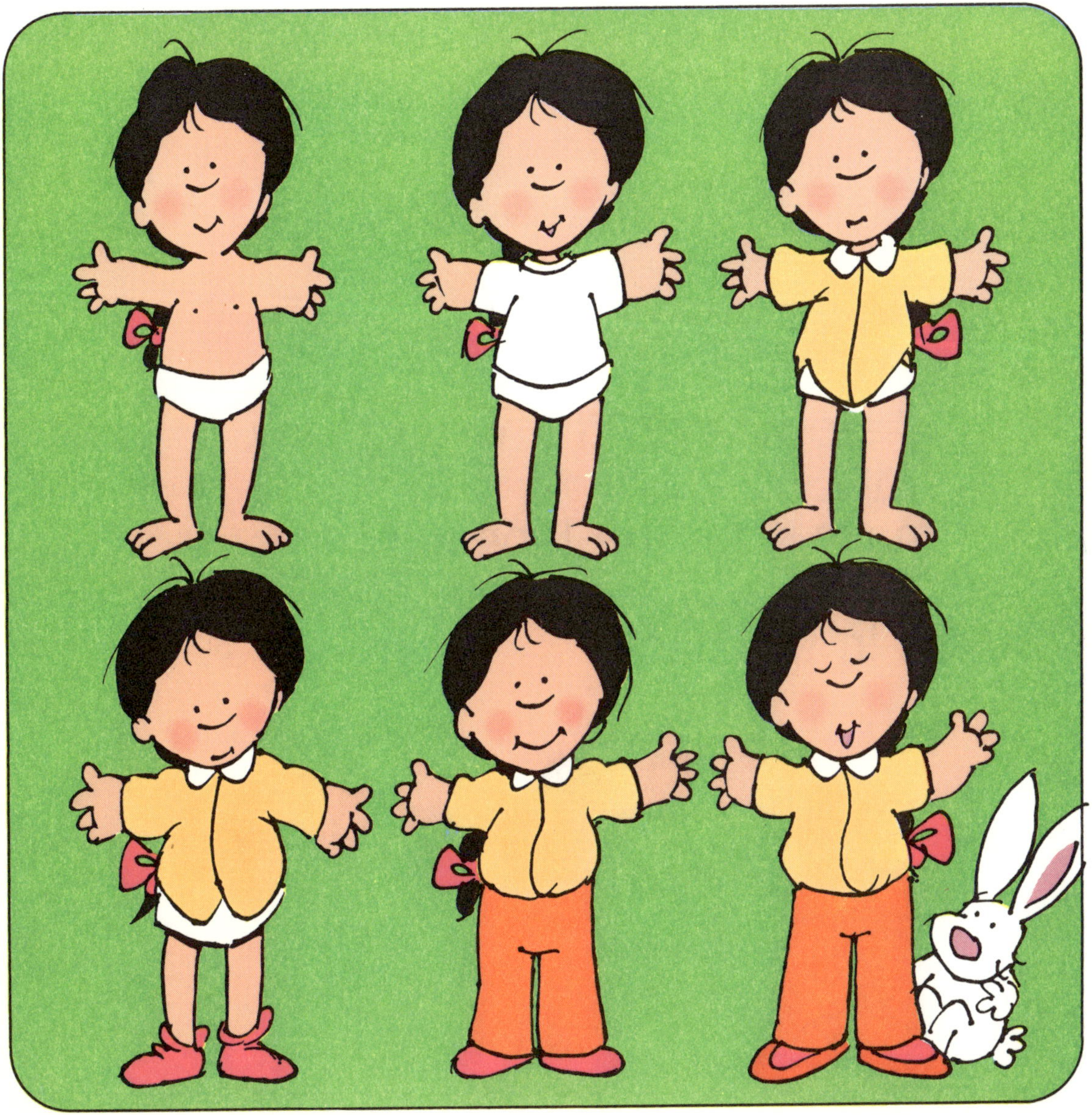

I do not want to put

my clothes on the wrong way.

I make sure the labels

are in the back.

Yes No No

I can put on my pullover top.

First, I put my head through

the biggest hole.

I make sure the label

is in the back.

I put one arm through one sleeve.

I put the other arm through

the other sleeve.

I pull the top into place.

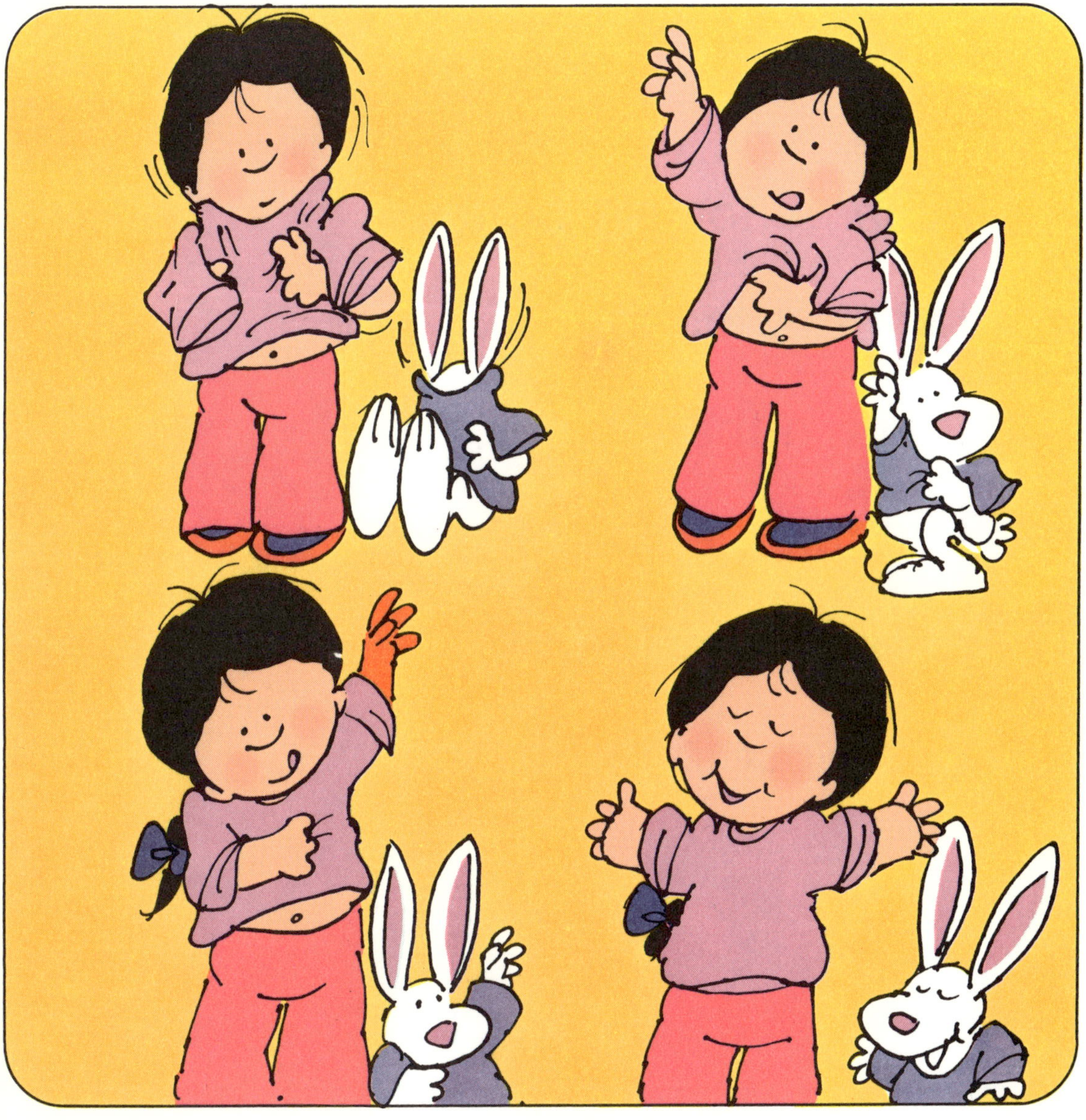

I can button my buttons.

I start at the top.

I button the top button.

I button the one below it.

I keep buttoning

until I get to the bottom.

Yes   NO NO

I can put my pants on.

I sit down.

I make sure the label

is in the back.

I put one leg through one hole.

I put the other leg through

the other hole.

I stand up.

I pull my pants up.

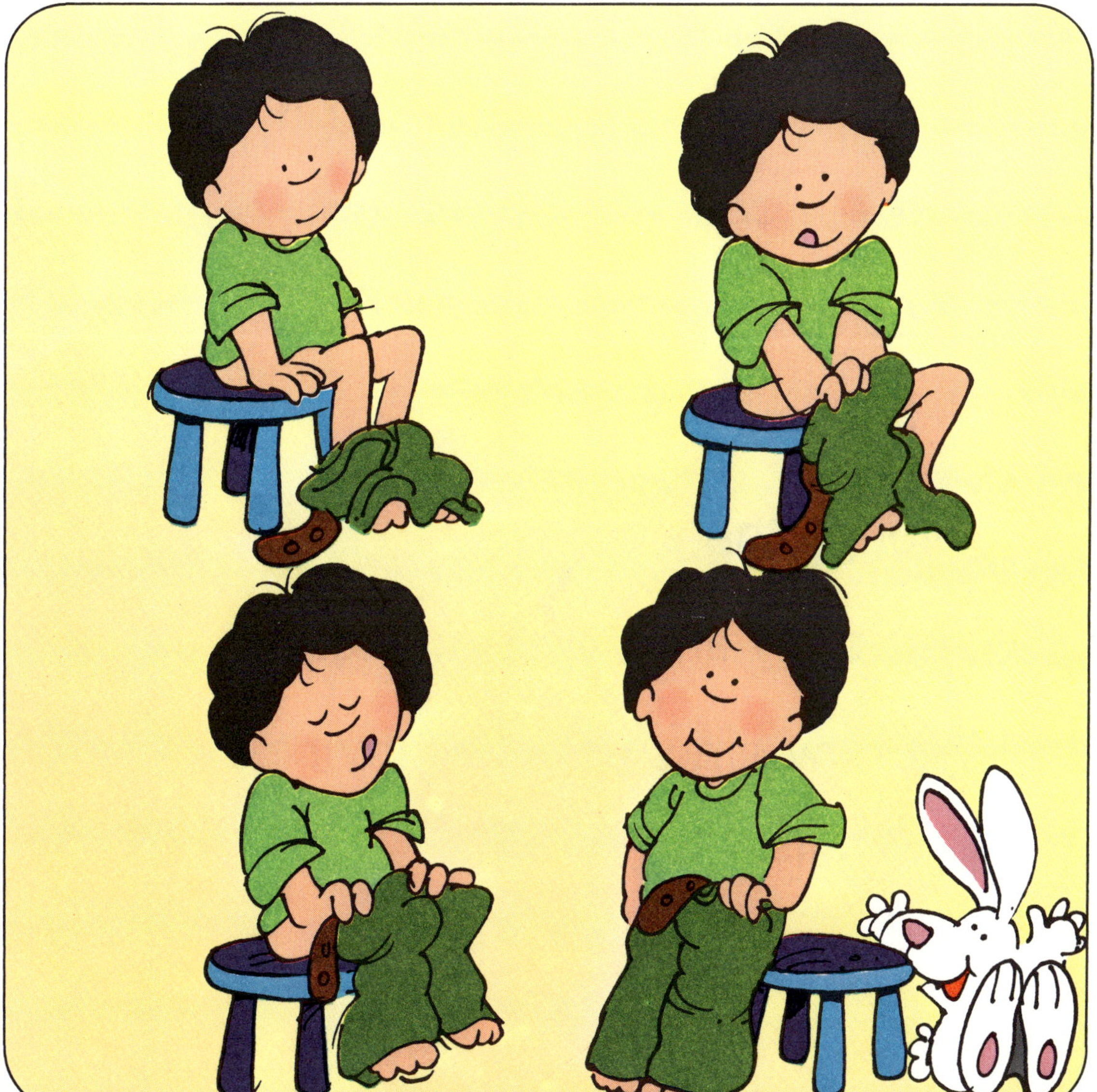

I can put my coat on by myself.

I lay my coat upside down.

I open it up.

I put both arms

through the sleeves.

I raise my arms over my head.

I put my arms down by my sides.

My coat is on!

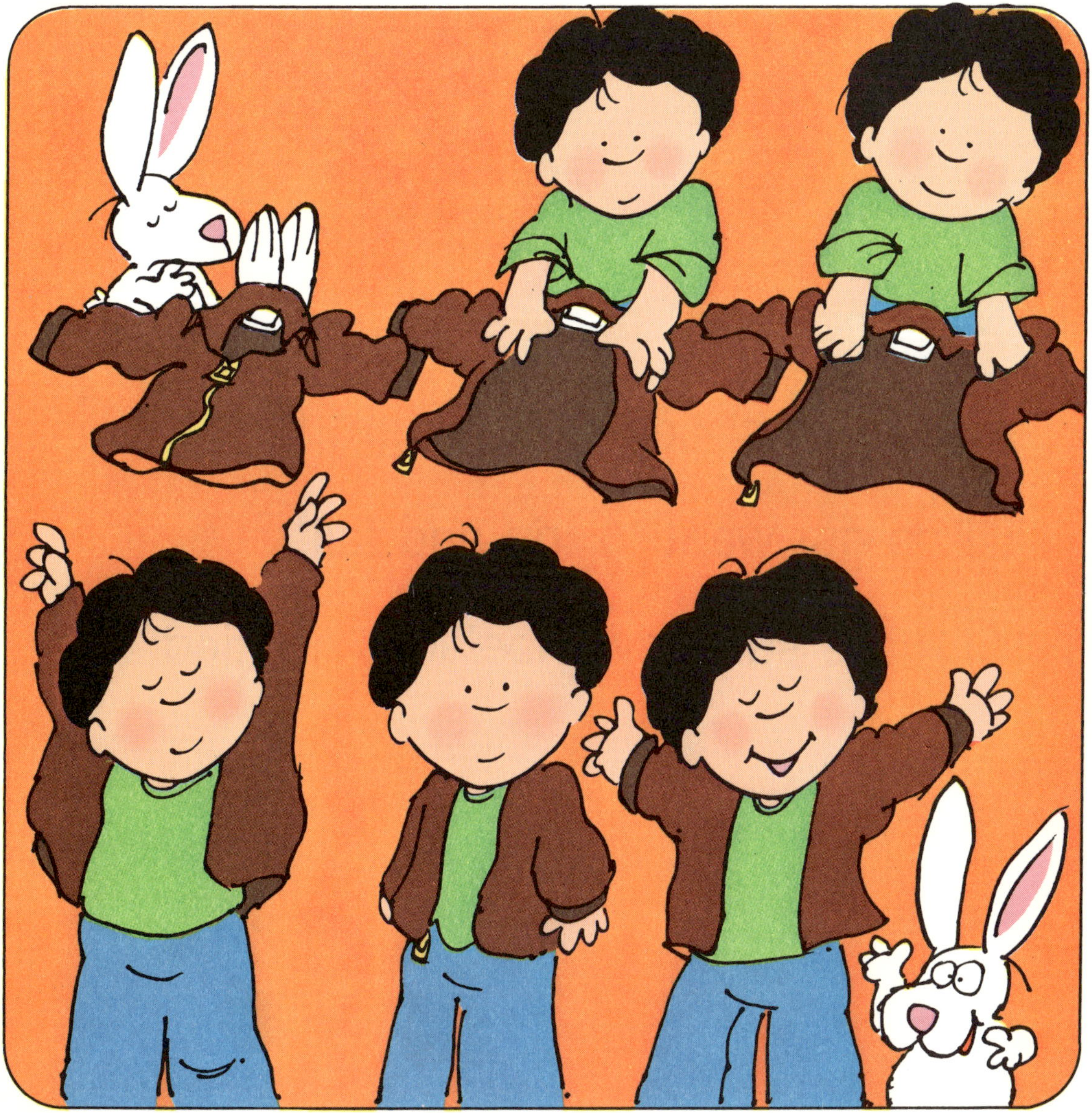

I do not want my feet to hurt.

I put my shoes on the right feet.

I do not want to trip and fall.

I make sure my shoelaces are tied.

NO NO   YES

I am dressed.

I feel good.

I look good.

I am ready to play.

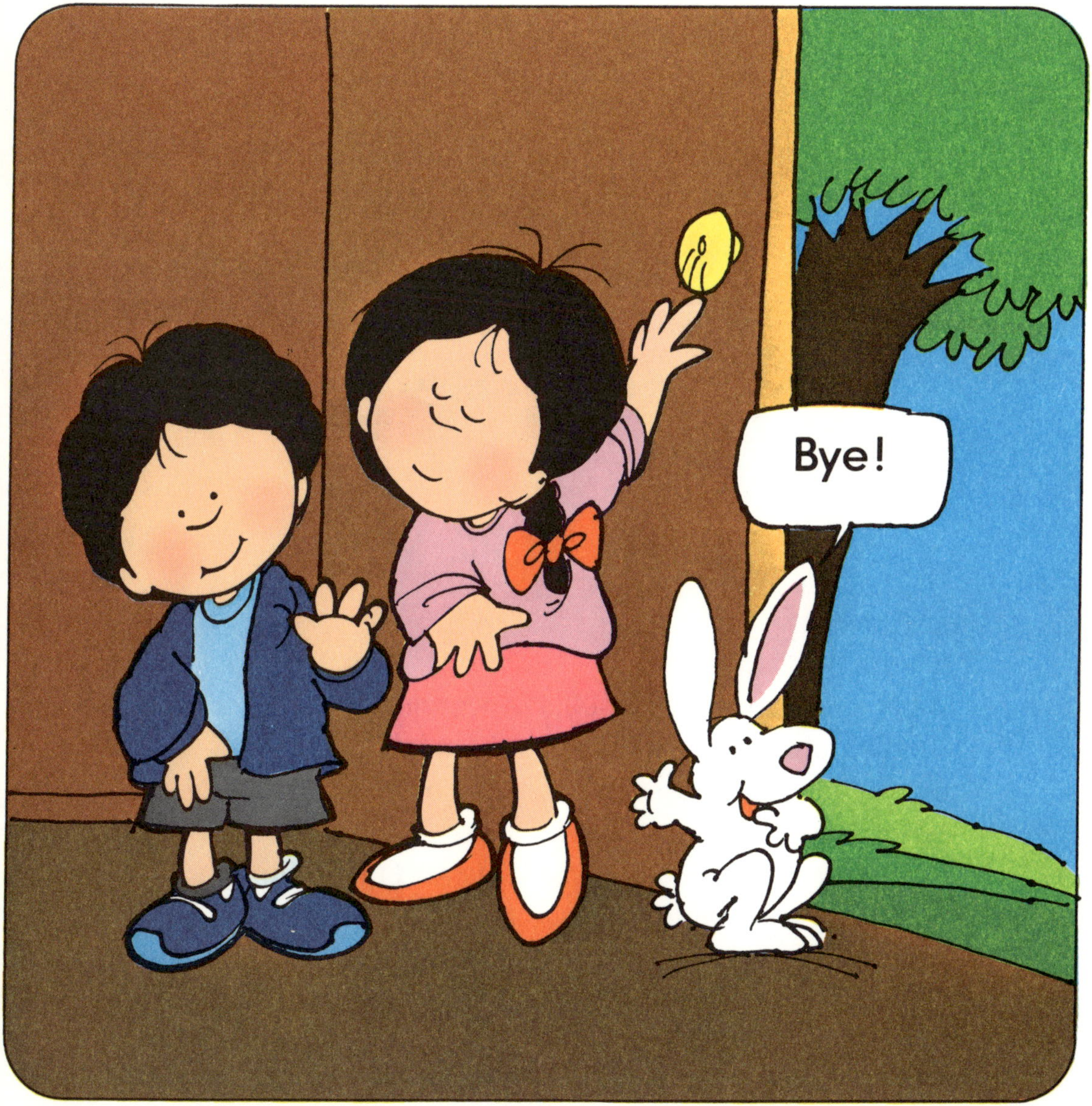
Bye!

helpful hints for parents about Getting Dressed

Dear Parents:

The purpose of this book is
- to show children the benefits of wearing clothing, and
- to teach children how to dress themselves.

You can best implement the purpose of this book by
- reading it to your child, and
- reading the following *Helpful Hints* and using them whenever applicable.

PUTTING YOUR CHILD'S WARDROBE TOGETHER

Here are some guidelines for putting together your child's wardrobe:
- Know your child's height and weight when you shop for his/her clothes as this is how children's sizes are determined.
- Purchase your child's shoes from a person who has had experience selling children's shoes. An experienced salesperson will know how to measure and fit your child properly. This should include measuring both of your child's feet.
- Remember that young children grow very quickly. Therefore your child will need only a few complete outfits and two pairs of shoes at a time.
- Try to revolve your child's wardrobe around three basic colors that go together. Navy or light blue, red, burgundy or pink, tan or yellow are usually good colors with which to work. A color-coordinated wardrobe will help your child look good in anything he/she chooses to wear.
- Purchase one kind and color of socks for your child. This will guarantee that every sock will have a mate.
- Select clothing that is made of washable, no-iron fabrics. Clothes that can be laundered and do not require ironing look neater and are easier to maintain.
- Try to choose clothing with zippers or Velcro closures instead of buttons or ties. Zippers or Velcro closures will be faster and easier for your child to use.
- Try to select one-piece outfits for your baby rather than skirts with blouses or pants with shirts. This is to accommodate the bulging tummy that makes it difficult for your baby to keep blouses or shirts tucked in and skirts or pants pulled up.

- Try to select skirts and pants with elasticized waists for your child. Skirts and pants that require belts are difficult to put on and keep up.
- Avoid getting clothes with long straps that can fall off the shoulders and annoy your child.

Here are some guidelines for choosing your child's sleepwear:
- Choose flame-retardant sleepwear for your child's safety.
- Dress your child in blanket sleepers on cold nights. They eliminate the need for a blanket because they cannot fall off or be kicked off during the night.

MAINTAINING YOUR CHILD'S WARDROBE

The following suggestions will help you and your child get the most out of the wardrobe you have put together.
- Before you put new clothes and shoes away, get rid of the ones that are too small or worn out. Clothes or shoes that are not being used can confuse a wardrobe and make it difficult to decide what to wear.
- Trade hand-me-down clothes with friends or relatives, or organize a clothes exchange at your child's day-care center, school, or church. Encourage parents to contribute hand-me-downs to the exchange, and allow them to take the used clothing their child can use immediately.
- Store your child's clothes in the lower drawers. This will enable him/her to reach the necessary clothes and get dressed.
- Put your child's clothes away in sets. A set of clothes should include a top, a bottom, and a pair of socks. This will help your child to put on clothes that coordinate.
- Rotate your child's clothes by putting the clean ones on the bottom of the stack. Encourage your child to take clothes off the top of the stack so that all of the clothes will receive equal use.

PROTECTING YOUR CHILD'S CLOTHES

Preserve your child's clothes by doing the following:
- Put iron-on patches inside the knees of each new pair of pants. This will prevent your child from wearing holes in the knees of the pants.
- Spray starch or fabric protector on knees, collars, and cuffs to prevent dirt from grinding into your child's clothes.

CLEANING YOUR CHILD'S CLOTHES

Here are some cleaning agents you can make with household supplies:
- **Cleaning Solution No. 1.** Mix together one-half teaspoon liquid dishwashing detergent and one tablespoon ammonia.
- **Cleaning Solution No. 2.** Mix together one cup liquid dishwashing detergent, one cup bleach, and two to three gallons water.
- **Cleaning Solution No. 3.** Mix together one cup bleach and two to three gallons water.

Extremely dirty clothes should be left to soak in one of these solutions for a few hours before they are laundered.
- **Stain Remover Paste.** Mix together one tablespoon unseasoned meat tenderizer and one tablespoon water.
- **Odor Eliminating Paste.** Mix together one tablespoon baking soda and one tablespoon water.

Apply one of these pastes on a stubborn stain or odor. Then roll up the article of clothing. Wait a few hours before you launder the article.

Here are some practical laundry procedures to follow:
- Add one-half cup baking soda to the wash and one-half cup white vinegar to the rinse to clean diapers and help prevent diaper rash.

- Add one-half cup baking soda to the wash to remove unpleasant odors from clothes.
- Add one tablespoon baby oil to the rinse to keep rubber pants soft.
- Rinse diapers a second time to remove the soap residue that can cause diaper rash or skin irritation.
- Button sweaters before washing them so they will keep their shape.
- Close zippers so they will not be damaged in the washer or dryer.
- Safety pin the two ends of a drawstring together so it will not come out in the wash.
- Put rubber pants in a mesh bag so they will not stick to the inside of the dryer.
- Remove fuzz balls from clothing (especially sweaters) with a dry sponge or coarse sandpaper.
- Remove surface lint and dirt from clothes with strips of masking tape.

Cleaning your child's shoes will be more effective if you do one or more of the following:

- Remove surface dirt on white shoes with rubbing alcohol. Then polish the shoes with white shoe polish.
- Rub a small amount of petroleum jelly on patent leather shoes. Then buff the shoes with a soft cloth.
- Cover scrapes on black patent leather shoes with a black felt-tip pen.
- Clean tennis shoes with a scouring pad and laundry detergent. Then rinse the shoes with water. White tennis shoes can be rinsed with lemon juice or bleach mixed with water.
- Dry tennis shoes with a towel. Then turn a hair dryer on high and put it in each shoe for approximately five minutes.

DRESSING YOUR CHILD

It will be easy to dress your child if you will follow these procedures:
- Dress your child **after** you dress yourself, when both of you are going out, so that he/she will not get mussed while waiting for you.
- Hang a mobile or toy over the changing table, or wear brightly colored plastic or wooden beads so your baby will be entertained while you change his/her diapers.
- Cover your boy with a cloth when you change his diaper to avoid being squirted.
- Place a pad under your girl when you change her diaper to keep the changing surface dry.
- Put fancy panties over your girl's disposable diaper for dress-up occasions.
- Place small objects in your child's hand before you put a long-sleeved shirt on him/her. It is easier to work a clenched fist through a sleeve.
- Guide your child's leg through a pant leg by reaching up through the foot hole. Cover the foot with your hand and gently pull it through the bottom opening.
- Teach your child to put on clothes in the following order:
    1. underpants
    2. undershirt
    3. socks
    4. top (blouse or skirt)
    5. bottom (skirt or pants)
    6. shoes

ADDITIONAL SUGGESTIONS

- Soften new clothes by laundering them before your child wears them.
- Stick diaper pins into a bar of soap or rub them on your scalp to make the pins slide into the diaper easily.
- Use masking tape when the tabs fail to work on a disposable diaper.
- Hem your child's skirt or pants quickly with masking tape.
- Glue a nonslip decal (commonly use in bathtubs) on the bottom of your child's first pair of walking shoes. This will provide traction for your child and will keep him/her from slipping.
- Sand the soles of new shoes to help your child avoid slipping.
- Place a strip of adhesive tape inside your child's shoe above the heel. This will keep his/her socks from slipping down into the shoes.
- Wet your child's shoelaces slightly so they will stay tied.
- Use two plastic bags for instant boots.
- Use two plastic bags over your child's shoes to make his/her boots slip on easily.
- Clip a notebook ring to your child's snowsuit zipper so that it will be easy to pull.